in and out of love

in and out of love

kim nguyen

Little Sunflower Press

ISBN-13: 978-1-7349437-0-2

Published by: Little Sunflower Press

www.kimntnguyen.com

to
my north star
in light and dark

release your heart
embrace love
in its entirety

in love

in and out of love

kim nguyen

to be in love is to love brilliantly. to love so intensely that your delicate heart skips more than a beat but an entire collection of wondrous songs. where your eyes gaze with exhilaration for each encounter. where your fingers tremble with anticipation for each touch. where your breath lingers with sweetness for each moment. for the one who is your north star and you theirs. for the one who is the reason why you've fallen and can't get up. for the one who is entirely and perfectly yours.

- to all who love

in and out of love

Adore

adore the *one* who captures your heart
with the sincerest admiration

the *one* who calms your worries
with a simple gentle touch

the *one* who makes you smile
with a soft whispered word

the *one* who takes your breath away
with a single innocent glance

Beauty

kim nguyen

of all the wonders
your eyes have gazed upon
to witness such beauty
to hold such grace
afraid to blink and make
the *one* ever invisible

each precious moment
flows with delight
an attraction expanding
beyond the physical
into one energy
illuminating two souls

Comfort

true to the core
of a natural essence
an effortless joy
an unfiltered lens
an open presence

nowhere else
except intimately
in between
the arms of the *one*
to embrace such bliss

Depth

kim nguyen

a million intricate threads
connect the layers of
the mind, body, and soul

revealing fears
inspiring desires
comforting worries
nurturing hope

to clearly see your reflection
in the complexities of another
a rare and beautiful encounter
with the *one* cut from
the same fabric of life

Excitement

kim nguyen

from the vivid rays
of sunrise to sunset
time stands still
yet passes by effortlessly

anticipation of waking up
to catch love
in its entirety
lying next to you

anticipation of falling down
to catch dreams
in their entirety
yet to come true

Fate

kim nguyen

visions once black and white
overflow with color
a vibrant journey ahead
of a future built together

strolling hand-in-hand
down tree-lined streets
aged hundreds of years
to destinations yet-to-be

the shades of sweetness
the grades of greatness
one life full of breadth
two hearts full of depth

Generosity

kim nguyen

an eternal gratitude for the *one*
patient and kind beyond measure

for accepting your flaws
an affection of your uniqueness

for seeing what you don't see
a long runway of your potential

for inspiring you to reach further
an expansion of your existence

Happiness

smiles shine
inside out
as laughter echoes
a connection grows

as soft skin glistens
a bright aura
radiates brilliance
in your presence

a love more
than enough
a love more
than whole

Inspiration

an unwavering belief
the *one* holds of you
to be the best of you
the *one* constantly
pushes you to the edge

where life breathes
where life pulsates
outside of the comforts
into the unfamiliar
where wildflowers bloom

Jubilation

kim nguyen

shout from the highest peak
the immensity of love for the *one*

the exclamations reverberate
echoes of undeniable joy

exhilaration caresses every corner
carving out waves of ecstasy

Kindness

kim nguyen

when you need it most
gestures of tenderness
strength of character

a shoulder to rest upon
a kind compliment
a long embrace

fingers intertwine
a hand to hold
so you never feel lost

in and out of love

Luck

once upon an ordinary day
turns out to be anything but
divine timing welcomes the *one*
to embark on this journey together

like the universe listens
to deliver what is asked
where the stars align up above
to shine down in your favor

Mesmerized

kim nguyen

unexpected moments pass by
timeless seconds etched in place

the glances of forever more
the conversations of late nights
the touches of endless pleasure

three precious words fallen
life to be lived never as before

in and out of love

Nirvana

an encounter from the past
reuniting familiar souls
every inch of you at ease
embracing the richness

even in stillness of silence
a truth left unspoken

warm breath against the skin
like sweet jasmine in the air
comfort in being yourself
no masks to ever wear

Open

lift up one another
to new perspectives
a view
without limits
without doubts

paint the blank canvas
beyond the lines
a scene
free to explore
free to create

Purpose

kim nguyen

to be the north star
for another
of another

put on this earth
to give strength
to be a force of life

put on this earth
to bring kindness
to be a saving grace

put on this earth
to show compassion
to love and to be loved

Quirks

kim nguyen

an eccentric couple
conversing in a language
all your own

to understand what
the *one* can only understand

nuanced interactions
like a kiss on a lone freckle
underneath your right eye

beyond casual curiosity
different yet the same

Romance

the unlikely surprises
like flowers just because
to brighten your day

the smallest acts
like opening the door
to value your worth

the thoughtful gestures
like handwritten notes
to replenish your heart

as if heaven grants
unspoken wishes
because of you

in and out of love

Sex

kim nguyen

a passionate act
turns kindle into flames
a magnetizing energy
draws two closer

a sensual kiss lands
on lips and in between
an intense sensation
intertwine bodies

a stimulating dance
comes to its peak
a calm washes over
pure bliss with the *one*

Transformation

kim nguyen

an incredible expansion
shaped by the *one*

desire not for perfection
but for a little less imperfect

an everlasting impression
shaped by the *one*

desire not for the possible
for the impossible exists

Undeniable

kim nguyen

an unwavering connection
vibrating through the earth

an illumination of passion
shimmering through the sky

mother nature as a witness
to a love so sweet and pure

Vulnerability

kim nguyen

let down your guard
the *one* will still be near
for every ounce of weakness
the *one* gives ten tons of strength

reveal pieces hidden in your shadow
craving the most radiant of light

embrace the discomfort
stand a while longer
for courage appears
in its unfolding

Wisdom

to comprehend the depths
of being human
all the mistakes
all the heartache
all the triumphs
perhaps all to really know
lies next to you
to learn and perfect
how to truly love another
and how to let another
truly love you

extra

kim nguyen

an extraordinary life
of ordinary moments

like a favorite song
landing on repeat

like a cup of coffee
brewed just right

like a funny joke
one after another

remarkably more
than what is enough

in and out of love

Yours

kim nguyen

one plus one equals
forever yours
complete and whole
as never before
two hearts sync
in beautiful harmony
orchestrate the beats
of vast possibilities

in and out of love

Zest

kim nguyen

an incredible adventure
through an uncharted course
pleasures eagerly await
with much anticipation

the sights
the smells
the sounds
the tastes
the touch

let the beauty of sunlight
transform into brilliant sunsets
with the *one* by your side
for all the days to come

art of love

in and out of love

to be out of love is to confront a profound sense of loss about who you are without another by your side. where you open yourself up to the raw emotions pouring in to face the darkness with strength. where you find true love within yourself before all else. where you believe again you are worthy to love and to be loved as hope begins to appear. trust another who radiates love just as brilliantly is ready and waiting on the other side. a place where hearts are no longer scared of getting lost because they will always remember their way home.

- to all who have loved and lost

Abandoned

kim nguyen

left alone in a senseless world
surrounded by senseless souls
when a promise to never leave
breaks and shatters so easily

for all you thought you knew
disappears suddenly like the *one*
scars buried deep inside crevices
time can only truly heal

you are not abandoned
the most important person
will always and forever be present
find lasting love within yourself
and you will never be alone

Bitterness

for taking away the future
once upon a time
and rupturing the bridge
of happily ever after

having to build walls
to hold back the hurt
waiting on the cracks
to inevitably break apart

don't let the pain overtake hope
for all that went wrong
let what may have to shatter
for the best things yet to be
to finally come together

Coldness

kim nguyen

cold towards another's touch
frozen in numb confusion
from what went so right
gone so wrong in an instant

believing no one cares
to lift you up above
from the depths below

ascend towards the warmth
above the hollow of your fears
breathe spark back to your spirit
reignite the fire flickering within

Depressed

not wanting to care
not wanting to feel
not wanting to try

wanting to cry
wanting to break
wanting to stop

longing for the days
to fast forward
to no longer face misery

longing for the days
to pause rewind
to erase painful memories

life happens
in temporary seasons
for evolving reasons

life happens
in unexpected lessons
for clarity of presence

Envy

kim nguyen

lost in between happy couples
yearning for what they possess
a connection made so naturally
a phenomenal intense energy

missing what lingers in the past
when days were on your side
a heart grasping beyond grief
desperate to return to normalcy

ignore comparison an ugly thief
lessening the true essence of you
discover the boundless wisdom
given in experiences of solitude

Frustration

kim nguyen

hateful words fuel the anger
towards the *one* once adored
who left a rawness
leaving you still shaking

wanting to hurt the *one*
who hurt you
the fights trigger
replays, flashbacks

end the battle in your mind
seeking to destroy what's left
protect what still remains
to rebuild all that awaits

Guilt

kim nguyen

guilty for trying again
chances to get close
but you pull away

you are too damaged
you don't deserve it
you are not enough

lovely you are enough

strong enough
confident enough
beautiful enough

to a level beyond
what you will
ever know

Hell

daydreams turn
into nightmares
fights against the
enemy within you

inner demons spread
hate and misery
nowhere to run
nowhere to hide

searching for a state
of numbness
where the pain
no longer exists

why should the *one* not suffer
when you have suffered enough
wanting to bring the *one* down
to the depths where you've fallen

but the deeper you go
the higher the climb
let the heaviness escape
let your soul rise again

Isolation

stranded on a deserted island
of your own creation
the vast waves of emotions
drowning you inside out
alone and afraid
uncertain of how to endure

you want to survive
you have to survive
you need to survive

swim against the tides
crashing down on you
no matter what the danger
push through the currents
for on the other side
a fierce survivor emerges

Jealousy

as the eyes wander
the mind wanders
innocent glances
passionate stares
tinder to sparks to fire

promises left in shambles

surrender the thoughts
release the hold
of the *one*
whose grip binds you
no more

Krockant

every chance life gets
a punch to the face
one last blow
sends you
to your knees

crawling, scraping, and struggling
to a corner of the ring for relief
believing no one stands by your side

find the will to persevere
take the smallest of steps
from the draw of surrender

live beyond a shadow of a doubt
open your battered eyes
to see all who have stood by you
giving you strength and courage
to finally fight back

Loneliness

kim nguyen

lying in an empty bed
reminders of what used to be
late night conversations
wrapped in each other's arms
until sunrise breaks through
with a good morning kiss hello
afraid of looming sunsets
longing for a kiss goodnight

be resilient in times faced alone
walking on these familiar roads
trust the journey will lead you
to understand and appreciate
the solitary moments
to quiet the mind
to nourish the body
to awaken the soul

Mistrust

kim nguyen

trust burns down to embers
leaving nothing but dust
how can you believe another holds
your best interest in mind
how can you believe you can place
your heart in their hands

without bruising it
without stabbing it
without breaking it

then another familiar with the pain
shines a mirror towards your core
to reflect the change
truth will bring
to reflect the hope
hidden deep inside

Nothing

kim nguyen

a disconnection
a profound void
a world once deemed
your bright and shiny oyster
shut completely
all turns black

pry open the shells
with your raw hands
for out of the darkness
radiates brilliance
reveal the treasures
eternally yours

Obsession

wondering how the *one*
is fine without you
wondering if the *one*
thinks the grass is greener
wondering how the *one*
constantly occupies your mind
when you don't occupy theirs

let your mind be still
let your heart be at peace
let your spirit be at ease
release the weight
off your shoulders
of a burden no longer
yours to bear

Paralyzed

kim nguyen

stripped naked
exposed bare
the body useless
from a broken heart

starved of control
of thoughts
of actions
of emotions

enrich yourself
with gratitude
with beauty
with kindness

an untethered soul
rises high
the body alive
from a light heart

Questions

kim nguyen

questions about your place
in the universe without
the *one* whose universe you made

questions with little answers
asking what you did
to deserve a glimpse of what used to be

leave the questions behind
give no substance
to what may never be known

time will fade the hesitations
breathe free of regrets
for life is to be lived not questioned

Resentment

kim nguyen

a decision by the *one* to walk away
a choice of giving up instead of getting up
a call for a tomorrow without you

brush yourself off and stand back up
you may be down but far from done
despite the wrongs know what's right

forgive the past
to fully be present
in the future for you

Skepticism

kim nguyen

you doubt if true love will show
its rare presence ever again
when it slipped from your hands
all seemed to suddenly vanish

the disappointments
discolor your belief
wary of other's intentions
without rhyme or reason

shed off the perspective
turning you against you
don't let words set in ink
seep into pages yet to be

keep the chapters pure
for rich new characters,
new narratives, and new scenes
to dance into splendid creation

Tired

tired of asking
tired of believing
tired of compromising
tired of praying
tired of sacrificing
tired of trying
tired of waiting
tired of feeling

feel alive
feel bold
feel confident
feel grateful
feel hopeful
feel inspired
feel passionate
feel worthy

Uncertainty

kim nguyen

anxiety tightly grips
the corners of darkness
not wanting to let go
of the fear that feeds it

searching for release
desperate to wake up
from this nightmare
of frantic loneliness

believe the radiant
light will break
turning blue nights
to bright days

believe the dotted
lines will connect
turning such doubts
to strong faith

Vexed

kim nguyen

on the edge of irritation
everything going against you
like the world makes fun of you
and everyone is in on the joke

shift your perspective
the world laughs at itself
at the unpredictability
of being human

forgive the imperfections
the expectations to be logical
in an illogical world
fallen upon all
who breathe
who try
who are

Weakness

cut down time and time again
no courage to start again
too fragile to try again

visions of the *one*
an illusion
of an us

throw yourself into the ashes
into the red fiery coals
rise like a phoenix

with such intensity
with such power
with such grace

soar over the horizon
more magnificent
than ever before

in and out of love

kim nguyen

the *one* who speaks
leaving remnants of empty words
the *one* who lingers
leaving your body tingling numb

the *one* who tortures
leaving scars that may never heal
the *one* who breathes
leaving only distant memories

release the fragile heart
sheltered and scared
back into the wilderness
to run and play like before

be open to another
ready and waiting
to make your heart
flutter once more

Yearn

kim nguyen

aching for the familiar
craving for the comfort
longing for the impossible
reliving only the positive
blurring out the negative

patience reaches out her hands
hold tightly as she leads you
where abundance flows
where desires flourish in a shade
greener than you have ever known

in and out of love

Zigzag

kim nguyen

trapped in a maze
desperate for escape
each step
fight or flight
each turn
dusk or dawn

it is time
sit in solitude to face
the intensity of emotions
until peace and forgiveness
enlightens a path
to finally set you free

to love

in and out of love

to love is to awaken an evolution of the rich essence of life between two breaths. where each encounter carries wisdom to guide kindred souls through the light and dark times. where the seeds of abundance are nourished to brilliantly bloom. where an imperfect love is greater perfected moment-by-moment while reveling in the one cut from the same fabric of life. the universe illuminates two silhouettes caught in a graceful dance as the moonlight glistens on delicate skin. with each enchanting step, love blossoms full of beauty in perfect progression.

- to all who have loved, lost, and yet still love again

Acceptance

kim nguyen

love holds no regard
to the skin she graces
building a home where
her heartbeat races

instantly falling
with spaces of light
patiently falling
with corners of night

catching your failures
no matter how heavy
counting your blessings
no matter how many

embracing the reality
of your mistakes
encouraging the hopes
of your one days

love unlocks her door
two enter her archway
taking the key to begin
one incredible journey

Boundaries

kim nguyen

rest dreams upon trees
next to each other
to extend their reach,
not to overshadow
but to feel the crisp air while
free to rustle in the wind

hold values close to earth
next to each other
to ground their roots,
not to over-tangle
but to feel the fresh soil while
free to savor the sun

lay desires into streams
next to each other
to explore their depths,
not to be lost
but to feel the pure water while
free to renew the soul

Choice

kim nguyen

a conscious decision
to receive love
to give love
and to be present
everyday
even in
the dark
the emotional
and the weary
turns of grey

Dedication

kim nguyen

love wavers
like tides of imperfection
drifting far from shore

hurtful words crash
into floods of shattered feelings
unmet expectations rush
into swells of throbbing pain

find peace in forgiveness
for the chaotic seconds
in the bitter moments
would otherwise bear regrets

love wavers
but does not break
finding land once more

Embrace

kim nguyen

love rises and falls
like the moon in her phases
embracing her shadow
and revealing her radiance

blow free the dust of
fleeting happy endings
eclipsing into darkness
whose time has come

chase the brilliant rays of
forging happy beginnings
gleaming into sunlight
whose time has just begun

in and out of love

Flourish

kim nguyen

all the pieces
exist in their entirety
set perfectly into place
completely whole
as you are

allow the happiness
you've created
you've fed
you've grown
to wildly flourish

a garden of abundance
sweetened by your
tender hands
ripe and ready
to savor with another

Gratitude

for
seeking
recognizing
embracing
strengthening
and falling
for love

for
bending
challenging
enduring
forgiving
and returning
for love

time and time again

in and out of love

Harmony

kim nguyen

each offbeat key
a chance to fine-tune
into a soul-stirring melody

until each unique chord
resonates flawlessly
into an exhilarating symphony

until each delicate note
blends intricately
into a captivating harmony

Infinity

kim nguyen

love is endless
like the night sky
full of stars
high above
shimmering
far below

wishes made
one-by-one
on the edge
of gentle lips
for countless
nights to come

Judgement

kim nguyen

accept the volumes of mistakes
neither came preassembled
or with an instruction manual

respect the pages of failures
confronting external pressures
and wrestling internal wars

honor the lines of flaws
reflecting an unpolished center
and shielding a hardened core

be the one
to love without hesitations
to love without reservations

Knowledge

kim nguyen

curiosity
to discover
the ins and outs
of another

each day
a new day
to unsurface
the nuances

their likes
their dislikes
their dreams
their fears

give love
open your heart
share love
expand your essence

in and out of love

Laughter

kim nguyen

a gift from the heavens
sounds of pure bliss
tickles in the belly
pour from the soul

a present to be shared
over and over again
contents so precious
no value can ever compare

Mindfulness

kim nguyen

to be aware of love is
to understand her every layer

from the fear of being seen
to seeing her true reflection
from the fear of being heard
to hearing her real intentions
from the fear of being touched
to feeling her deep emotions

see reasons for her falls
find ways to catch her
hear reasons for her dreams
find ways to guide her
feel reasons for her wonder
find ways to amaze her

each layer more exquisite
than the one before

Nourish

kim nguyen

give love sunshine breaks
take her out in the rain
dance with her
nap with her
feed her
catch her when she falls
pick out the thorns when she tumbles
kiss the bruises when she hurts
wish her a good morning
tuck her in good night
treat her well in all the ways
for she will forever do the same

Originate

kim nguyen

the honeymoon phase
extends past just
a temporary stage

long standing creations
attract like vibrations
magnets to the manifestations

positive intentions flow
into outgoing destinations
shapes future jubilations

sparked interactions elevate
into sensational connections
crystalizes to golden perfection

Patience

strands of a worn-out brush
dipped in a bright, bold shade

anxious fingers tremble
afraid of making a mistake

strokes of intention
vivid with colorful splatters

touches of creation
vibrant with lively matter

lines of masterpieces
exquisitely defined

Quality

kim nguyen

seconds limited in quantity
held in time

be fully present
instead of barely there

be engaged in conversations
instead of shallow exchanges

be fulfilled in experiences
instead of hollow occasions

rich breaths
sweetened in life

Respect

kim nguyen

treat each other with dignity
above what the other
may give themselves

value each other with integrity
for who you stand for
is who you stand by

honor each other with sincerity
hold with high esteem
one worthy of the universe

Selfless

kim nguyen

anticipation
without
expectations

in every chance
in every way

as the body quivers
offer your warmth
in times of shiver

as the soul quakes
offer your comfort
in times of ache

as the heart quiets
offer your patience
in times of silence

love
without
regard

Trust

kim nguyen

a foundation of commitment
strong enough to hold the core,
tend to the cracks
before they break

walls of loyalty
sound enough to hold the space,
tend to the memories
before they fade

windows of honesty
clear enough to hold the rays,
tend to dusted panes
before they haze

shelter to weather the storms
when the clouds darken,
sanctuary to relish the days
when the sun heartens

Unity

kim nguyen

love each other as you are
in the present

less by the definition
of the past

less by the prediction
of the future

by the two basking
in this absolute moment

Verge

the first one to share parts of you
when opening up
makes you scared

the last one to speak gracefully
a reminder of
someone who cares

the courage to show up fully
when uncertain of
who will be there

the faith to leave the familiar
to grow beyond
what is known

the heart to love more than another
a weakness only few have
the strength to show

Worthwhile

the sacrifices
the compromises
the fights
the tears

fade into shadows
as the brilliance from

the laughter
the affection
the joy
the cheers

brightens the days
and enlivens the nights

eXpansion

kim nguyen

drift away from the flock
like curious birds of nature
through the pristine clouds
across the sky of wonder

release your tethered wings
shielded and scared
soar into the vast heavens
higher than ever dared

extend your mighty feathers
against comforting fears
graze the crisp amber horizon
draw the unencumbered air

Years

kim nguyen

treat love like a verb
and less like a noun
an action to be taken
and less a thing to be found

beyond an emotion
of momentary reaction
witness the transformation
of a natural progression

from crawl to walk to run
like a delicious evolution
ripens the flavors of time
from days to years to life

Zen

kim nguyen

love at her best
is free of resistance
full of allowance
to be as she is
purely present

let difficulties
come and go
like visitors
passing
brief in stay

let blessings
gently linger
like best friends
reminiscing
twilight away

being human is happiness.
being human is heartache.
being human is heaven.
being human is hell.

when you are in love, savor the incredible moments dancing between two souls. cherish love in its entirety. when you are out of love, open up to the raw emotions pouring in. rediscover love within you. trust another will find you when you're ready and not a moment sooner. when you truly love, embrace the awakening illuminated through the light and dark times. radiate the brilliance to love and to be loved.

the words i've shared reflect the hope and wisdom of a life rich with joy and layered with sorrow. the poems represent the strength i've gained which have carried me here today, and i pass forward to help carry you to all the beauty that awaits. thank you for experiencing this journey with me into the depths of being human.

- to all who breathe

kim nguyen

kim nguyen is a vietnamese-american writer,
artist, and creator. through her poetry, she shares
the depths of human connection, discovering and
expressing the narratives of life with undertones
about love. her creative calling blossomed late
in life although the seeds were planted long ago.
at 13 years of age, she wrote her first love poem
about heartbreak. twenty-seven years later, she has
written 78 love poems about heartbreak and hope.
she is committed to inspiring others through her
artistic vision and creations.

- about the author